OBJECTIVE TRUTH

THE GREAT AMERICAN DIVIDE

By Dennis W. Hicks — © 2018

www.HisTruthWorks.com

9 781300 155010

TABLE OF CONTENTS

What Divided America?
Objective Truth:

"We shall soon be in a world in which a man may be howled down for saying that two and two make four, in which people will persecute the heresy of calling a triangle a three-sided figure, and hang a man for maddening a mob with the news that grass is green."
— G.K. Chesterton (1874-1936).

I t's obvious that America is becoming increasingly divided but what is the fundamental cause of the division? Americans have always had differences but those differences did not divide us. From the founding of our nation, Americans have come from different nations, different ethnicities, different religions, different races, and different political ideologies; but we were all united as proud Americans.

America is quickly becoming two nations under one name. Now there are arguments even about what it means to be an American. The two Americas cannot coexist. Like all tribes, they will argue, then they will hate with irrational hatred, then they will war. There will be no peace until one faction conquers the other.

Something is increasingly dividing us into a form of irrational tribalism with all of tribalism's disadvantages. Tribes are social structures that compete with, demonize, separate from, and even war with the other tribes.

Each tribe views the whole of society through the lens of their own social identity and core values. Now we have gender tribes, skin-color tribes, ethnic tribes, white male tribes, feminist tribes, political tribes, religious tribes, and social-justice tribes. All of them are irrational and dangerous.

What has changed? What is the proximate cause that transformed the traditional American "melting-pot" into this street fight between tribes? If it's not our differences, what is the real Great American Divide?

The dangerous divide is over the existence or non-existence of objective truth.

That is the fundamental dividing line; that is America's battleground and has been for the last 100 years.

Belief, or non-belief, in the existence of objective truth will determine how one views history, science, and the nature and the purposes of both society and government. It will determine one's moral standard, one's political ideology, one's ability to reason, one's view of individual rights, one's views on education, and one's views of the significance of history. There is a lot at stake on whether one believes that objective truth exists and can be discovered, is immutable, and universally applies to every time, every place, every circumstance, every culture, and every person.

The rejection of the existence of objective truth will lead to a rejection of American traditional values, rejection of the founding principles that were the cause of American exceptionalism, rejection of the authority of the American Constitution, and rejection of the authority of the Bible.

This is serious business and we should take the time and make the effort to understand how the rejection of objective truth became an issue in America. Who promoted the rejection of objective truth? Why were they successful? And why did they want this cultural change in America?

WHAT IS OBJECTIVE TRUTH?

Objective truth is discoverable and verifiable by the scientific method. Objective truth is something that remains verifiably true no matter what we believe. Objective truth is discovered in the nature of the things we investigate. It is the nature of the Law of Gravity that it works the same throughout time and geographical setting. It is the nature of humans that they must be governed or they will create chaos— what we call "anarchy," the absence of government.

In this investigation into the cause of America's divisions, we assert that Natural Law and traditional standards of morality are objective truth. Both are rooted in nature and reason, both are discoverable and verifiable using the scientific method.

Secular-progressives (and in history, despots, and statists) redefine "truth" as that which successfully brings about the desired result. Anthropogenic Global Warming and Multiculturalism are examples of this substitute definition of truth: They both are designed to control and transform society—and they are treated as truth because they are successful at achieving that end. Both theories require the denial of objective truth; both are pseudo-science masquerading as truth.

Objective truth is reasonable. The ancient tools of Logic and Rhetoric are designed to operate in the arena of objective truth and aid in discovering truth. Both Logic and Rhetoric have been de-emphasized or removed entirely from our public education curricula because they will reveal the non-truth of the secular-progressive ideologies that have come to characterize modern public education. Sadly, most parents and churches have remained silent and have provided no better alternatives, choosing to avoid conflict by compromising objective truth.

WHAT IS NATURAL LAW?

Natural Law is the objective truth concerning the purposes and scope of real authority that is delegated by God to individuals, families, the church, and human government. All authority is held by God; if any authority exists anywhere, it belongs to God (See Matthew 28:18).

God has delegated very narrow authority, with defined purposes and scope, to the God-designed institutions that are created for the security and happiness of mankind: Families, the church, and government. The delegated authority will be forfeited if the one exercising the authority exceeds either the defined purposes or scope of that authority.

The specific purposes and scope of authority delegated to individuals, families, church, and government are spelled out in the Bible and have been observed and explained in antiquity. Even before the New Testament was written, intelligent observers have investigated and largely understood Natural Law. Natural Law is universal, like the law of gravity it applies to all mankind throughout all time and in all cultures. It is discoverable by all and forms the basis of a just society.

Socrates, Plato, and Aristotle deduced that Natural Law is a moral theory of jurisprudence; that law should be based on morality and ethics—based on what is true. In his *Rhetoric*, Aristotle argues that aside from "particular" laws that each people-group has set up for itself, there is a universal "common law" or "higher law" that is according to nature (*Rhetoric* 1373b2-8).

The American colonists understood their duty to throw off British rule and establish a new government based on Natural Law because England had violated the scope and purposes for human government as defined in a law superior to British law—Natural Law. Those specific violations of Natural Law are spelled out in our *Declaration of Independence*.

Chapter One—Setting the Stage

The fixed values
of American Colonists:

Historians agree that three necessary conditions permitted the founding of America. This was the first time in history that a nation was founded by choice, not by force, or war, or political revolution:

1) **A particular Opportunity:** An opportunity to form a new nation existed in North America among the British colonies.

2) **A particular Leadership:** Wise and learned leaders existed that were able to bring the majority of the population of the colonies together in understanding they had a moral duty to throw off British rule because it had violated the purposes and scope of government's authority under Natural Law. They had a duty to form a new limited government that would protect individual rights to life, liberty, and property.

3) **A particular People:** The people were well educated and had a common rational understanding of the fundamental principles that defined their values. (If you doubt they were well educated, read the Federalist Papers, if you can, that were written to the average farmer in Upstate New York). There was a common understanding of the principles of virtue and Natural Law among the people. They trusted

their leaders, that they were wise and would form a new government consistent with the principles of Natural Law and human nature.

From this fertile ground sprung the most powerful most prosperous nation in history.

For America's first 150 years, the people were purposefully educated and they loved freedom, truth, and virtue. They were convinced of the existence of objective truth, so they sought after truth and expected to find it. They studied the Bible to find truth; they sought to stand on the shoulders of giants so they studied history and the philosophical writings of antiquity. They learned Greek and Latin so they could understand the teachings of dead white men like Aristotle, Cicero, and Seneca. They studied and taught the apostle Paul's teachings on Natural Law in the Bible as it is applied to the individual, the family, the church, and human government. They wanted to understand the unalterable principles of law and human government, so they read Montesquieu and Locke in their homes.

They understood that public and private virtue were necessary to sustain a popular (Republican) form of government, that without an anchor of virtue the republic would ultimately devolve itself into tribalism followed by tyranny. The objective principles of virtue and Natural Law were learned in their homes and were reinforced in their schools and their churches. French historian Alexis de Tocqueville observed that it was almost impossible to find an

American who would deny the existence of objective truth or admit they disbelieved the Bible.

The American Revolution was not caused by over-taxation, it was caused by England's violations of "the Laws of Nature and Nature's God"—*The Declaration of Independence*. It was a religious issue: England's government had violated the scope and purposes of human government defined by Natural Law in the Bible. By those violations, England forfeited her authority over the colonists and the colonists understood why England's authority over them was lost.

It was the pulpits of American preachers that brought about the revolution by teaching Biblical principles of authority and the clearly defined scope and purposes of human government under Natural Law. The British gave those courageous and patriotic preachers the derogatory title of the 'Black Robed Regiment' because of how their courageous public stand on the principles of Natural Law motivated the citizens. In her book, *The New England Clergy and the American Revolution,* Alice Baldwin summarized the role the American clergy had in the revolutionary war:

> "There is not a right asserted in the Declaration of Independence which had not been discussed by the New England clergy before 1763. The Constitutional Convention and the written Constitution were the children of the pulpit."
> — Historian Alice M. Baldwin, *The New England Clergy and the American Revolution,* 1918.

The current battle in American politics is centered, not in a dispute over government's expanding bureaucracy (the agent of progressive ideologies), but over something more fundamental: Is Natural Law objectivey true, or are we free to cast off its restraints on the scope and purposes of government to achieve social justice?

The real debate is not over politics, but over the applicability of specific principles: Are a just civilization, freedom, and standards of morality merely social constructs designed by men, or are they objectively defined in the Bible and conferred by God? Who is the giver of freedom? Is freedom "endowed by our Creator," or is government the definer and granter of freedom? Were our Founders right when they declared that standards of virtue and the principles of Natural Law are indispensable in a Constitutional Republic?

Our Founders warned us that our very existence as a Constitutional Republic rests on the true principles of Natural Law and virtue among the people:

> "Public virtue cannot exist in a nation without private, and public virtue is the only foundation of republics. There must be a positive passion for the public good, the public interest, honour, power and glory, established in the minds of the people, or there can be no republican

government, nor any real liberty: and this public passion must be superiour to all private passions." —John Adams, letter to Mercy Warren, 1776.

"[T]he propitious smiles of Heaven, can never be expected on a nation that disregards the eternal rules of order and right [Natural Law], which Heaven itself has ordained. The foundations of our national policy will be laid in the pure and immutable principles of private morality; and the preeminence of free government, be exemplified by all the attributes which can win the affections of its citizens, and command the respect of the world."

— George Washington, First Inaugural Address, 1789.

"Bad men cannot make good citizens. It is impossible that a nation of infidels or idolaters should be a nation of freemen. It is when a people forget God that tyrants forge their chains. A vitiated [impaired] state of morals, a corrupted public conscience, is incompatible with freedom. No free government, or the blessings of liberty, can be preserved to any people but by a firm adherence to justice, moderation, temperance, frugality, and virtue; and by a frequent recurrence to fundamental principles." —Patrick Henry (1736 - 1799).

"No people will tamely surrender their Liberties, nor can any be easily subdued, when knowledge is diffused and Virtue is preserved. On the Contrary, when People are universally ignorant, and debauched in their Manners, they will sink under their own weight without the Aid of foreign Invaders." —Samuel Adams (1722 - 1803).

"A general Dissolution of Principles & Manners will more surely overthrow the Liberties of America than the whole Force of the Common Enemy. While the People are virtuous they cannot be subdued; but when once they lose their Virtue they will be ready to surrender their Liberties to the first external or internal Invader. How necessary then is it for those who are determin'd to transmit the Blessings of Liberty as a fair Inheritance to Posterity, to associate on publick Principles in Support of publick Virtue." —Samuel Adams, 1748.

These men were not radicals in their day; they were the national leaders who proclaimed and defended the values commonly held by the people. But they would be considered intolerable radicals outside of the mainstream of today's America. They would be denounced and vilified by academia, the news media, the entertainment industry, and every progressive social-justice warrior. Their wisdom would be declared "hate speech" to be silenced by force, if necessary. Darkness always hates the light.

How did it happen that the bedrock principles and values that made American great are now openly and vociferously denied and rejected? De Tocqueville would be shocked and so would our Founders.

The fault may be found in the general rejection and abandonment of objective truth from which the immutable principles of virtue and Natural Law are learned. Today, de Tocqueville would have little difficulty in finding someone who denies the existence of objective truth, who disbelieves the Bible and rejects our founding principles as being out of date, unable to address the complex needs of a modern society. Almost any American college campus would be a target-rich environment for such disbelief.

He would have considerable difficulty though, in finding citizens who can accurately define the principles of Natural Law or the fundamental attributes of personal and public virtue. Once commonly understood, these are largely unknown in America today. What brought about such pervasive ignorance?

Robert C. Winthrop (1809-1894—a descendant of Governor John Winthrop) was the first governor of Massachusetts Bay Colony. He served as a Representative and Senator from Massachusetts and Speaker of the United States House of Representatives.

The following is from an address he gave at the Annual Meeting of the Massachusetts Bible Society in Boston, stressing the necessity of religion's moral restraints in America's Republic:

"All societies of men must be governed in some way or other. The less they may have of stringent State Government, the more they must have of individual self-government. The less they rely on public law or physical force, the more they must rely on private moral restraint. Men, in a word, must necessarily be controlled, either by a power within them, or by a power without them; either by the word of God, or by the strong arm of man; either by the Bible, or by the bayonet. It may do for other countries and other governments to talk about the State supporting religion. Here, under our own free institutions, it is Religion which must support the State" —Robert Winthrop, May 28, 1849.

Such wisdom would not be permitted on many of America's college campuses today. But the subject and purpose of this booklet is to answer the question, What is the cause of the rejection of America's founding principles and values that are essential to preserving "Life, Liberty, and the Pursuit of Happiness?"

Chapter Two–Setting the Stage

The ideologies of American Secular-Progressives:

I t was shortly after the Cuban Missile Crisis in 1962, the clash between Russian communism and American hegemony in the region, that Congress investigated and published the purposes and strategies of communists in America. The resulting document, *Current Communist Goals*, was published in the *Congressional Record*. Among the strategies of American communists was to distort and discredit the bedrock principles of American culture:

Congressional Record--Appendix, pp. A34-A35
January 10, 1963
Current Communist Goals
EXTENSION OF REMARKS OF HON. A. S.
HERLONG, JR. OF FLORIDA
IN THE HOUSE OF REPRESENTATIVES
Thursday, January 10, 1963

20. Infiltrate the press. Get control of book-review assignments, editorial writing, policymaking positions.

21. Gain control of key positions in radio, TV, and motion pictures.

22. Continue discrediting American culture by degrading all forms of artistic expression.

23. Control art critics and directors of art museums. "Our plan is to promote ugliness, repulsive, meaningless art."

24. Eliminate all laws governing obscenity by calling them "censorship" and a violation of free speech and free press.

25. Break down cultural standards of morality by promoting pornography and obscenity in books, magazines, motion pictures, radio, and TV.

26. Present homosexuality, degeneracy and promiscuity as "normal, natural, healthy."

27. Infiltrate the churches and replace revealed religion with "social" religion. Discredit the Bible and emphasize the need for intellectual maturity which does not need a "religious crutch."

28. Eliminate prayer or any phase of religious expression in the schools on the ground that it violates the principle of "separation of church and state."

29. Discredit the American Constitution by calling it inadequate, old-fashioned, out of step with modern needs, a hindrance to cooperation between nations on a worldwide basis.

30. Discredit the American Founding Fathers. Present them as selfish aristocrats who had no concern for the "common man."

31. Belittle all forms of American culture and discourage the teaching of American history on the ground that it was only a minor part of the "big picture."

32. Support any socialist movement to give centralized control over any part of the culture--education, social agencies, welfare programs, mental health clinics, etc.

40. Discredit the family as an institution. Encourage promiscuity and easy divorce.

41. Emphasize the need to raise children away from the negative influence of parents. Attribute prejudices, mental blocks and retarding of children to suppressive influence of parents.

American secular-progressives and the Democratic Party have adopted the communist's banner and their ideological strategy.

What would be required to convince the American people that the above Socialist goals were desirable, even necessary?

One has only to look as far as the prominent founders of American Progressivism to answer that question. The foundational ideology that produced American Progressivism was introduced long before the American Communist Party was formed, but they share the same root, goals, and strategies to transform American governance and culture.

The present administrative state in America and the current cultural-political divide are products of the political ideologies of the Progressive Era (1890-1920). Believing America's foundational principles of virtue and government under Natural Law were not absolute, but were outdated and unable to address the complex issues of a modern society, the Progressives believed the purposes and scope of government were not fixed objective truths; they needed to be defined anew for each historical epoch.

The men who are considered the founders of American Progressivism are John Dewey, Frank Goodnow, Woodrow Wilson, Theodore Roosevelt, and Herbert Croly. These men all had the same fundamental belief, a common thread that was foundational to their political and cultural ideologies: the repudiation of objective truth and particularly America's founding principles.

They all rejected the existence of objective truth, and thus relativism was introduced into American thinking, education, and politics. The Constitution was now considered a "living document," not a fixed immutable framework for government. Natural rights conferred by "Nature's God" were replaced with social rights conferred by a scientific and expertly run government. Modern Progressive "Social Warriors" spring from these malignant roots:

Observe how each of the following American Progressive founders denied the existence of objective truth (Chapters 3 through 7).

Chapter Three—John Dewey (1859-1952):

As the leading Progressive scholar from the 1880s onward John Dewey, who taught mainly at Columbia University, devoted much of his life to redefining the idea of education. His thought was influenced by German philosopher G.W.F. Hegel, and central to it was a denial of objective truth and an embrace of historicism and moral relativism. As such he was critical of the American founding."— *The U.S. Constitution: A Reader*, Hillsdale College, 2012.

Hegel (1770-1831) believed the regulatory state, not the individual, will produce the culture. John Locke (1632-1704) taught the individual is sacred and the individual defines the culture, that governments exist to protect the individual's rights. Herein is a succinct description of the current Conservative-Progressive divide in American politics.

Dewey denied the laissez-faire economic principles of Adam Smith, that if men are left unhindered to develop their own life and property, they will collectively improve society as a whole. Dewey believed that was an outdated principle, not an objective truth; that government could better control the means of economic production than independent individuals:

"The only form of enduring social organization that is now possible is one in which the new forces of productivity are cooperatively controlled and used in the interest of the effective liberty and the cultural development of the individuals that constitute society. Such a social order cannot be established by an unplanned and external convergence of the actions of separate individuals, each of whom is bent on personal private advantage."

— *"Liberalism and Social Action*, John Dewey, 1935.

Dewey denied the existence of objective natural rights of the individual, especially that those rights were superior to social legislation. Dewey believed a rigid rule of law hindered social progress:

"The earlier doctrine of 'natural rights,' superior to legislative action, has been given a definitely economic meaning by the courts, and used judges to destroy social legislation passed in the interest of a real, instead of purely formal liberty of contract. Under the caption of "rugged individualism" it inveighs against all new social policies." —ibid.

Dewey maintained that the founding principles should be confined to the founding era:

"... their own [the Founder's] special interpretations of liberty, individuality and intelligence were themselves historically conditioned, and were relevant only to their own time. They put forward their ideas as immutable truths good at all times and places;

they had no idea of historic relativity, either in general or in its application to themselves." "... they were themselves absolutist in the social creed they formulated." —ibid.

Dewey rejected the notion that the founding principles, God-conferred individual rights, and the limits on human government imposed by the Bible's Natural Law, that they were objective and timeless truths. He taught they were merely ideas that "were relevant only to their own time." Dewey taught that arguments for the immutable nature of the founding principles restricted the ability of government to produce "effective liberty - a function of the social conditions existing at any time" and imposed a "regime of despotism ... at the expense of genuine social order, unity, and development."

Dewey's rejection of objective truth, even the Bible's absolute truth, led him to reject the foundational principles of virtue and Natural Law. He worked to replace the Founder's principles of individual freedom with government-imposed social planning:

"Organized social planning, put into effect for the creation of an order in which industry and finance are socially directed in behalf of institutions that provide the material basis for the cultural liberation and growth of individuals, is now the sole method of social action by which liberalism can realize its professed aims." —ibid.

The current bureaucratic despotism in America (called the "Swamp") is the realization of Dewey's progressive ideologies: That the objective truths of virtue and Natural Law are considered irrelevant, and that government actions form the best culture, not virtuous citizens.

CHAPTER FOUR—FRANK GOODNOW (1859-1939):

Frank Goodnow, president of Johns Hopkins University and the first president of the American Political Science Association, helped pioneer the idea that separating politics from administration was the key to progress ... he addresses the need to move beyond the ideas of the founders."— *The U.S. Constitution: A Reader*, Hillsdale College, 2012.

Goodnow disagreed with the Bible and America's founders in that he disagreed that man was endowed at the time of his birth with certain unalienable natural rights; that man was primarily an individual and only secondarily as a member of human society: "Such a theory, of course, has no historical justification."— *The American Conception of Liberty*, Frank Goodnow, 1916. He denied the Bible's teachings and the teachings of antiquity on the matter of unalienable rights of the individual.

Goodnow claimed the founder's doctrines of natural rights were not rooted in objective truth, but "were at that time the result of the then existing social conditions, and like most such theories were also an attempt to justify a course of conduct which was believed to be expedient." —ibid.

He claimed the natural rights defined in the Declaration of Independence were rights granted by law, "not natural rights inherent in man," "not by his

Creator, but rather by the society to which he belongs." "Social expediency, rather than natural right, is thus to determine the sphere of individual freedom of action." —ibid.

Goodnow denied the Bible was objective truth but he (rightly) perceived the doctrine of natural rights came from the people's religion: "The religious and moral influences in this country ... all favored the development of an extreme individualism. They emphasized personal responsibility and the salvation of the individual soul." "Everything, in a word favored the acceptance of the theory of individual natural rights." —ibid.

Goodnow, influenced by the theory of evolutionary development, rejected the permanence and immutability of the doctrine of natural rights. He believed social and scientific progress have outrun the founder's natural rights theory: "Changed conditions, it has been thought, must bring in their train different conceptions of private rights if society is to be advantageously carried on." "We no longer believe as we once believed that a good social organization can be secured merely through stressing our rights." —ibid.

Goodnow observed that "Many universities have in the past been the homes of conservatism." —ibid. He and John Dewey made it their mission to change that by promoting the denial of the existence of objective truth in American education.

CHAPTER FIVE—THEODORE ROOSEVELT (1858-1919):

Theodore Roosevelt's ascension to the presidency in 1901, upon the assassination of William McKinley, marked the emergence of Progressivism on the national scene. From trust-busting to railroad regulation, Roosevelt sought to expand federal power over a large swath of the American economy." — *The U.S. Constitution: A Reader*, Hillsdale College, 2012.

Both Theodore Roosevelt and Woodrow Wilson agreed concerning the limitations of government imposed by the Constitution and the founder's doctrine of Natural Law. Both Roosevelt and Wilson sought to expand the authority of the president beyond the scope and purposes defined in Natural Law. Roosevelt believed the president should have complete freedom to do whatever meets the current needs of the nation:

> "My belief was that it was not only his right [the president's] but his duty to do anything that the needs of the Nation demanded unless such action was forbidden by the Constitution or by the laws. Under this interpretation of executive power I did and caused to be done many things not previously done by the President and the heads of the departments ... I did greatly broaden the use of executive power." — *Making an Old Party Progressive*, Theodore Roosevelt, 1913.

Roosevelt had cast off the objective truths concerning the limits and purposes of government authority in Natural Law. He took specific steps to expand the power of the presidency to turn government into a power to shape the nation and the American culture into his vision:

> "I was bent upon making the Government the most efficient possible instrument in helping the people of the United States to better themselves in every way, politically, socially, and industrially." "I wished to make this democracy industrial as well as political ..."
> —ibid.

Roosevelt believed the Constitution should be considered malleable, not restricting the government from doing what it thought was expedient or best:

> "I believed in invoking the National power with absolute freedom for every National need; and I believed that the Constitution should be treated ... to aid a people in exercising every power necessary for its own betterment, and not as a straitjacket cunningly fashioned to strangle growth." —ibid.

President Barack Obama had a similar view of the malleability of the U.S. Constitution:

Democratic presidential candidate Barack Obama described the U.S. Constitution as having "deep flaws" during a September 2001 Chicago public radio program, adding that the country's Founding Fathers had "an enormous blind spot" when they wrote it.

Obama also remarked concerning the Constitution, "But I think it is an imperfect document, and I think it is a document that reflects some deep flaws in American culture, the Colonial culture nascent at that time." —From a panel discussion that aired on Chicago's WBEZ-FM on Sept. 6, 2001, titled *"Slavery and the Constitution."*

Presidents Roosevelt, Wilson, and Obama swore an oath to uphold and defend the Constitution of the United States, but all three denied the Constitution was a strict rule of law, an immutable declaration of objective truth.

CHAPTER SIX—WOODROW WILSON (1856-1924):

After earning a Ph.D. in both history and political science at Johns Hopkins University, Woodrow Wilson held various academic positions, culminating in the presidency of Princeton University. Throughout this period he came to see the Constitution as a cumbersome instrument unfit for the government of a large and vibrant nation. In his speeches, delivered during his successful campaign for president in 1912, ... called 'The New Freedom', [he] put forward the idea of an evolving or 'living' Constitution' ." — *The U.S. Constitution: A Reader*, Hillsdale College, 2012.

Wilson understood our Constitution was crafted on known laws, "the laws of Nature and of Nature's God," that constrained the government by built-in checks and balances. He believed our governmental structure was inherently flawed: "Government is not a machine, but a living thing. It falls, not under the theory of the universe, but under the theory of organic life. It is accountable to Darwin, not to Newton." — *What is Progress?* - Woodrow Wilson, 1913.

Wilson also believed the immutable principles of the Declaration of Independence were outdated because they did not address "the questions of our day." —ibid.

Wilson was enchanted with the socialist ideologies of Western Europe and believed America should follow their example: "From the other side of the water men can now hold up against us the reproach that we have not adjusted our lives to modern conditions to the same extent that they have adjusted theirs." —ibid.

From our advantage of hindsight, Wilson thought it wise for America to follow Cyprus, Spain, and Italy to their economic and cultural doom.

Repudiating the objective truth of the natural rights of the individual, he believed "communities are supreme over men as individuals." —*Socialism and Democracy*, Woodrow Wilson, 1887. "The thesis of the state socialist is, that no line can be drawn between private and public affairs which the State may not cross at will; that omnipotence of legislation is the first postulate of all just political theory." "[M]ust not government lay aside all timid scruple and boldly make itself an agency for social reform as well as for political control?" —ibid.

Like Roosevelt, Wilson advocated concentration of power in the President at the expense of the Legislative branch of government. He wanted "A president whom it trusts can not only lead it, but form it to his own views." "His office is anything he has the sagacity and force to make it." —ibid.

President Obama's Executive Orders and bypassing Congress' approval of treaties are taken from Wilson's socialist playbook: [The President] "may even substitute his own orders for acts of Congress which he wants but cannot get." —ibid.

Woodrow Wilson's presidency is referred to in history as the Progressive Era. Once casting aside objective truth, like Dewey and Goodnow before him, the Constitutional constraints of government under Natural Law and the natural rights of man, are forced to give way to a president who can form the nation into his own vision.

Wilson's activist socialist administration gave us The Federal Income Tax (1913); the Federal Reserve System (1913): the Seventeenth Amendment that reduced state representation in Congress by changing the appointment of Senators by state legislators to popular vote (1913); and the growth of government bureaucracies operated by "experts."

CHAPTER SEVEN—HERBERT CROLY
(1869-1930):

I n his book [*Progressive Democracy*, 1915], Herbert Croly, a leading Progressive theorist and founder of *The New Republic* magazine, criticizes the Founders' fear of tyranny of the majority and rejects their idea that government exists to protect individual rights." — *The U.S. Constitution: A Reader*, Hillsdale College, 2012.

Like Dewey, Goodnow, Roosevelt, and Wilson, Croly rejected the objective truths of Natural Law and the principles of America's Founders and advocated the replacement of our Republic with a "direct government," a true Democracy, what our Founders referred to as "mob rule."

In Croly's view, the Founders chose a representative government because that was the only reasonable choice in their day; but times have changed in a way that now enables a better democracy to replace our Republic:

[Our Representative Republic] "was imposed by the physical and technical conditions under which government had to be conducted. Direct government did not seem to be possible outside of city or tribal states ..." "[R]epresentative government ... was prescribed by fundamental economic and social conditions." — *Progressive Democracy*, by Herbert Croly, 1915.

"In the twentieth century, however, these practical conditions of political association have again changed, and have changed in a manner which enables the mass of people to assume some immediate control of their political destinies." "The adoption of the machinery of direct government is a legitimate expression of this change." "Pure democracy has again become not merely possible, but natural and appropriate." —ibid.

Croly had abandoned the existence and authority of objective truth and therefore viewed the great American experiment as a "long and barren alliance with legalism." —ibid.

With no compass of objective truth to guide him, Croly advocated something that has already been achieved by modern Progressives: Collaboration between the legislative and executive branches of government, placing lawmaking and the executor of the laws in essentially the same hands.

In our day, Congress has delegated its lawmaking authority to federal bureaucracies in the Executive Branch of government; what our Founders explained will ultimately lead to tyranny.

Croly wanted to reorganize the executive and legislative branches into one collaborative power:

"An organization of the executive and legislative powers, which will give increased energy to both of them and which is adjusted to their cooperation both one with another and with a sufficient measure of direct government, is what is needed and must be contrived." —ibid.

The abandonment of objective truth, as displayed in Natural Law, the Declaration of Independence, and the Constitution, is the proximate cause of the exponential growth of the "Fourth Branch" of government: The Federal bureaucracy, the "Deep State."

"Pick any three letters of the alphabet, put them in any order, and in the acronym, you will discover an unnecessary federal agency."

—Economist Milton Friedman.

Chapter Eight—Setting the Stage
The Pathologies of the American Truth-Divide:

Until America's Progressive Era, the immutable principles of Natural Law and virtue were commonly taught and defended in society and polity. The principles were taught as objective truth in our homes and were reinforced in our schools and churches. Our elected officials were expected to be living examples of virtuous principled living. Our founding documents enshrined the limits of government under Natural Law and were considered to be permanent structures for American governance.

The development of personal and public virtue was expected to be a common goal of every American citizen—even for all immigrants. Immigrants at that time wanted to become Americans; they wanted to embrace the traditional values that made America a great nation.

What has the rejection of objective truth produced in America over the last 100 years?

Public Educational Pathologies:

In the late 19th and early 20th centuries, Progressive ideologies advanced unopposed in American culture, particularly in academia among the intellectual elite. That war has been already lost. The wholesale rejection of objective truth has been largely achieved in our schools, championed by the public media, with only a very few exceptions.

When the government infringes on the educational authority of the family, both government and family are weakened and the children are harmed. The destructive changes in American education made over the last 100 years are, at its root, a battle over authority. Who will have authority over our children? Parental authority and the influences of religion over children are enemies of the statists' coveted authority over everything. Progressive Statists seek to make the state the center of society. All other authorities must be made subordinate to the state, even family authority, and especially religious authority.

The efforts by government and academia to remove religion and parental influences from public education have produced very costly failures: They have given us a "values-free education," which is, in reality, an exchange of traditional American values rooted in objective truth for Progressive relativistic values, resulting in a cultural moral decline.

They have given us an educational system that transformed a homogeneous society with shared values into divided tribes with conflicting core values. There can be no community without shared values.

The American educational system once produced greatness in the students, but no more. The change was the direct result of progressive ideologies forced into our schools by an intrusive government that tied progressive educational forms and philosophies to government money for schools. New goals for public education in America, that removed the goal of developing virtue, were defined in *The Cardinal Principles of Secondary Education*, published by the U.S. Department of the Interior Bureau of Education in 1918.

The indoctrination of America's youth in the utilitarian-pragmatic ideologies of progressivism had begun in earnest. A new kind of American, called "the right kind of human capital," became the intended product of government-run education. The former educational goal of equipping students for a virtuous life of serving God and their fellow man was purposely replaced with inferior goals.

American public education enacted the progressive philosophies of John Dewey, the "father of progressive education," and co-author and signer of *The Humanist Manifesto*. Dewey explained his rationale for radically changing American education:

> "You can't make Socialists out of individualists — children who know how to think for themselves spoil the harmony of the collective society which is coming, where everyone is interdependent."– John Dewey, Quoted by Ann Coulter in, *Godless: The Church of Liberalism*, 2006.

While the new controlling document for American education was being written (*Cardinal Principles*), by 1917, the administration of American schooling was in the hands of a leftist elite group referred to as "The General Education Board," comprised of representatives of Rockefeller, Carnegie, Harvard,

Stanford, the University of Chicago, and the National Education Association. Their collective goal for education in America was to impose on the youth the idea of subordination: the new goal became to produce a large and compliant workforce. The Board believed that unless America's culture of Yankee entrepreneurs could be transformed, at least among the common population, the immense capital investments in mass production and internationally competitive businesses would not be justifiable.

Students needed to be trained to think of themselves as employees competing for the favor of management, not as self-determined free agents. The ability of Americans to think as independent producers who could achieve their dreams by their own hands needed to be curtailed through long-range social engineering and behavioral modification. The desired educational product in America became a less creative, unthinking workforce, content to perform specific tasks in return for a regular paycheck.

The General Education Board warned us in 1918 they intended to produce an inferior educational product in American public schools:

"In our dreams, we have limitless resources and the people yield themselves with perfect docility to our molding hands. The present education conventions fade from their minds, and unhampered by tradition, we work our own good will upon a grateful and responsive rural folk. We shall not try to make these people or any of their children into philosophers or men of learning, or men of science. We have not to raise up from among them authors, editors, poets or men of letters. We shall not search for embryo great artists, painters, musicians nor lawyers, doctors, preachers, politicians, statesmen, of whom we have an ample supply...The task we set before ourselves is very simple as well as a very beautiful one, to train these people as we find them to a perfectly ideal life just where they are. So we will organize our children and teach them to do in a perfect way the things their fathers and mothers are doing in an imperfect way, in the homes, in the shops and on the farm." —*General Education Board, Occasional Papers*, No. 1, 1913, p. 6.

The new corrupt and harmful educational goals should have been opposed by parents, and Christian leaders, who sounded the alarm, but they were not— they were silent. The <u>New York Times </u> devoted an editorial to condemn The General Education Board's utilitarian educational philosophies, calling them "radical and dangerous."

"Unblushing materialism finds its crowning triumph in the theory of the modern school. In the whole plan there is not a spiritual thought, not an idea that rises above the need of finding money for the pocket and food for the belly ... It is a matter of instant inquiry, for very sober consideration, whether the General Education

Board, indeed, may not with the immense funds at its disposal be able to shape to its will practically all the institutions in which the youth of the country are trained.

If this experiment bears the expected fruit we shall see imposed upon the country a system of education born of the theories of one or two men, and replacing a system which has been the natural outgrowth of the American character and the needs of the American people ... The plans of the General Education Board call for careful examination."

—*The New York Times*, January 21, 1917.

The Pathologies of a Bureaucratic Government:

A PRINCIPLE: The self-governing virtues advocated in the Bible, and the specific purposes and limits on government defined in our Constitution, are both necessary to maintain liberty and order.

To the progressive elite, the ideologies and principles of our Founders are the problems, not the solutions, because they restrain impetuous change and Progressives believe all change is progress. They believe the principles of Natural Law and virtue are overly restricting and the Constitution too confining to achieve social justice in a changing modern society.

To Progressives, there is no "settled truth" because there is no objective truth. Those who believe in absolutes, like the *Bible* and our Constitution as law, are pitted against those whose disbelief in objective truth causes them to view such absolutists as fringe radicals: "[I]t's not surprising then they get bitter, they cling to guns or religion or antipathy toward people who aren't like them."

—Barack Obama, Speech at a San Francisco Fund Raiser, April 2008.

A PRINCIPLE: Breaching the natural checks and balances of equal authorities in Natural Law will result in the concentration of powers in one authority and collusion between authorities.

Upon rejecting objective truth in government, the checks and balances among the three branches of our federal government, as defined by our Constitution, have now been replaced by collusion between the once co-equal and interdependent branches for the expressed purpose of expanding and controlling an administrative state run by experts.

Congress, designed to be a deliberative slow-moving law-making branch of government, has lost its way by colluding with the executive branch to create and manage an ever-expanding government bureaucracy that wastes the taxpayers' money and rules by arbitrary laws. Congress has become a mere administrator of an ever-expanding bureaucratic despotism in America.

The once-common understanding that public spending and public debt were moral issues receded with the growth of the administrative state. Now, there are no limits on spending; virtue and morality are no longer budgetary considerations. There is no basis for distinguishing between what government can do and what government should do.

Since Congress has delegated its law-making authority to bureaucracies of the Executive Branch (an act foolishly supported by the Judiciary), the authority and coercive power of government have been widely distributed to an unaccountable government bureaucracy that remains in power no matter who wins elected offices. Government bureaucracies now wield the powers delegated to Congress by "We the people," and the people have no say in the matter, but powerful special interest groups do.

Our Founders warned us that under the Bible's principles of Natural Law, the natural checks and balances that constrain government would prevent collusion among the competing branches of government and between the federal and state governments. Any collusion would usher in tyranny by expanding government beyond its defined scope and purposes until the government becomes the most significant institution among the people, unchallenged by family or religion. The servant would become the master, ever-expanding its rule and power over the people until citizens become subjects.

The progressive transformation of American politics is a conscious repudiation of the immutable principles on which our nation was founded, with the goal to expand the role of government. It must be obvious that the more government does, the easier it is for elected officials to do favors for voters and donors, enabling them to win elections and stay in power. The political Nanny State did not merely evolve as the culture evolved; it was the intended result of a strategy to transform America and pillage the citizen's property.

Early progressives meant to usher in a new order that was appropriate for the more sophisticated industrial age. They believed the government ought to be involved at every level of society as the instrument of social change, aided by new scientific knowledge and the development of an administrative bureaucracy populated by experts.

Only good men will make good governors, and only a government constrained by the principles of Natural Law can produce both liberty and order.

When "We the people" reject objective truth we will be ruled by the bayonet, by government force. Tribalism and chaos will be our lot.

When "We the people" defend the principles of Natural Law in our families, churches, and government; when we develop virtue in our homes and reinforce virtue in our schools and churches; only then will we be able to reverse the horrific damage inflicted on our families and our nation by Secular-Progressive non-truth.

CHAPTER NINE—THEN AND NOW.
CONCERNING EDUCATION AND MATURITY:

The recognized founders of American Progressivism all had rejected the existence of objective truth as they developed their worldview and their political ideologies. That rejection of objective reality is a common thread, a common cause, among those who reject America's founding principles and traditional values.

It should be no surprise that evangelical Christians and Mormons predominantly identify with political conservatives and the Republican party; while liberal Christian groups and atheists predominantly (69%) align with political leftists and the Democratic party. One set believes in the existence of objective truth, the other does not — *10 Facts about atheists*, by Michael Lipka, Pew Research Center, June 1, 2016.

As Americans turn away from God, the Bible, and objective truth, they increasingly think and act in the realm of non-reality. Atheists seldom (never) look to the Bible or religious writers in history concerning questions of right and wrong; they primarily look to modern science on those questions. Non-religious people tend to reject the possibility of objective standards of morality, and they believe a person can be moral and live a noble life without them. Therefore, atheists overwhelmingly favor same-sex marriage (92%) and legal abortions (87%) —Pew Research.

According to the Pew Research Center, the number of self-proclaimed atheists in America has more than doubled between 2007 and 2014, as have the number of self-proclaimed agnostics during the same period. The trend away from objective truth is obvious and frightening. —Pew Research.

• THEN—CONCERNING EDUCATION AND MATURITY:

To paraphrase Alexis de Tocqueville: America was great because America was good; and if America stops being good, America will stop being great. To "Make America Great Again" (MAGA) one must make America good again.

What's at stake in our child-rearing is the character of the next generation of citizens: Will they be wise and virtuous or ignorant and evil? Will they be selfish or will they aspire to a noble life of serving God and their fellow man? Will they be able to reason, able to make rational grown-up decisions, or will they become useful idiots, mere prey to sophists and propagandists? Elitists, who consider themselves superior in intellect, power, and position, can only successfully control careless people who will sell their freedom for a mess of pottage—people who think unrestricted license is liberty and expect the government to take care of them while they live irresponsible indolent lives.

"The philosophy of the classroom will be the philosophy of government in the next generation." —Abraham Lincoln.

Early American education produced some of the most capable, most successful, and competent statesmen, merchants, scientists, intellectuals, and entrepreneurs the world has ever known. They raised great businesses, great families, great leaders, good reputations, notable scholars, and built a great nation.

In colonial America, it was the home that was the first schoolroom and the most influential lecture hall. There, affection and intellect came together; mother-love and learning to reason joined forces. It was in the home schoolroom future military officers, statesmen, merchants, poets, leaders in industry and science learned of religion, virtue, grammar, logic, and rhetoric —primarily at the knees of their parents.

This nature of the American colonial family produced the great Americans de Tocqueville reported of in his historical books, *Democracy in America*. Those great Americans were not an accident or coincidence of time. They were the intended product of virtuous families; the intended result of the considerable investment to raise wise and virtuous children.

For America's Founders (among whom John Adams is named) the principles of Natural Law defined a moral order that can and should guide human life and government—a moral order that is consistent with human nature and reason.

John Adams' wife, Abigail Adams, claimed no formal education ("I was never sent to any school") but her letters show a fluency of multiple languages, classical poetry, history, and principles of government that would put most modern post-graduate students to shame.

Having never set foot in a school classroom, Abigail was able to teach their children (among them, John Quincy, the 6th President of the United States) to reason, read and write, math, classical poetry, Latin, French, English, and Greek languages. She taught and modeled virtue: courage, discipline, industry, prudence, purity of words and actions, truthfulness, steadfastness, and the love of religion, morality, and liberty. She taught them the Christian religion was the foundation of leadership and patriotism, "for a true patriot must be a religious man." She taught and modeled daily prayer and taught practical reliance on God as the Ruler over the affairs of men: "The refuge of the believer, amidst all the afflictive dispensations of Providence, is that the Lord reigneth, and that He can restrain the arm of man." – *Familiar Letters of John Adams and His Wife Abigail Adams*, Charles Francis Adams, 1875. (Recommended reading).

The primary source of learning private virtue and morality is the family. Their first public expression occurs in churches and schools. Here also should be the powerful role models that affirm and demonstrate what it means, practically, to be an educated, virtuous and moral person. American citizens' ability to self-govern, their ability to make the moral choices necessary for effective self-determination, depends on their families teaching and modeling virtue and morality, and upon their churches and schools, as allies to parents, affirming and reinforcing those principles necessary for a secure and happy society.

• NOW—CONCERNING EDUCATION AND MATURITY:

It's a startling and revealing comparison to juxtapose early American families with modern families to see how we have "progressed," having abandoned the objective standards of virtue and the Natural Law principles of our predecessors.

In early America, most young men graduated from college and began their business careers by about age 18.

According to recent studies, when a parent, teacher, counselor, law-enforcement officer, or judge is speaking to a thirty-year-old they must treat him as a child. Today's lengthy and mythical childhood has certain measurable attributes that would explain why most young American males are not mature enough to get married and raise a family, or even to find and retain employment.

Syndicated columnist and author, Diana West, summarizes the marks of our adolescent culture in her book, *The Death of the Grown-Up: How America's Arrested Development Threatens Western Civilization;*

> "Adolescence has become, and this must not be missed, the goal of our culture. Somewhere along the way, we ceased to be a culture where kids aspire to be adults and became a culture where adults aspire to be kids."

The Marks of an Adolescent Culture:

What are the marks of a culture with a dominant adolescent mindset? Not surprisingly, they are precisely what we have come to expect from adolescents themselves.

1. Demand for immediate gratification, spiraling credit card debt, addiction to new technologies, bouncing from church to church, abandoning marriages—the list goes on and on.

2. Absence of long-term thinking about life and the world. Ours is a culture largely ignorant of economic theory, political distinctions, or the rules of logic.

3. Motivated by feeling rather than truth. Truth is murdered by pooled and polled ignorance.

4. Wanting grown-up things without growing up. Ironically, despite our addiction to all things adolescent, we still expect to be treated like adults. "Don't tell me what to do," we say. "Every opinion matters" and "treat me with respect," we add.

5. Expecting bailouts. And once we accept adolescence as normal, we are then forced to excuse poor behavior.

6. Focusing on appearance rather than depth. Seen in everything from fascination with celebrity to the way presidents and churches are chosen. Cultures that choose style over substance quickly become silly cultures."

— Commentary on *The Death of the Grown-Up: How America's Arrested Development Threatens Western Civilization*, by Diana West, http://www.allaboutworldview.org/adolescent-culture.htm.

Our adolescent culture has rid us of adult role models, particularly where they are needed most, in families and churches. There, the men often look and act like boys. Their dress, stunted language, fascination with technological gadgets, their aversion to the hard work of learning Truth, and purposelessness in life all expose their startling immaturity.

Chapter Ten—Then and Now.
Concerning objective Truth:

Our Founders devised our Constitutional Representative Republic with a deep understanding of human nature and Natural Law. From their knowledge of history, they understood the dangers that had destroyed all previous attempts at popular government. The separation of powers doctrine designed into our Constitution (derived from the immutable principles of authority under Natural Law), and the understanding that governors must themselves be governed, was commonly understood by almost all of the colonial citizens.

What we call traditional American values today were rooted in the objective standards of morality, family life, human nature, and self-control found in the Bible. The glue that bound the disparate religious beliefs of the American colonists was their common belief in the objective truth of the Bible, including the biblical doctrine of Natural Law that defined the purposes and scope of authority delegated to the individual, family, church, and government.

Historian Alexis de Tocqueville observed the way Americans prevent despotism from arising is for Americans to cherish and try to sustain their commonly-held moral and religious beliefs.

"As for me," he concludes, "I doubt that man can ever support a complete religious independence and an entire political freedom at once." If "he has no faith, he must serve, and if he is free, he must believe. If they wish to retain their freedom to govern themselves, a democratic people must strive to sustain the common religious culture that underlies their common moral convictions." —Alexis de Tocqueville, *Democracy in America*, 1840.

Alexis de Tocqueville examined America before America's "Golden Age," the beginning of her greatest expansion of freedom and prosperity. He determined America's virtue, and her unprecedented freedom, were not inherent in her culture (after all, they were largely British immigrants), but in her common Christian religion:

"In the United States the sovereign authority is religious ... there is no country in the world where the Christian religion retains a greater influence over the souls of men than in America, and there can be no greater proof of its utility and of its conformity to human nature than that its influence is powerfully felt over the most enlightened and free nation of the earth. The safeguard of morality is religion and morality is the best security of law as well as the surest pledge of freedom." —ibid.

America never had a uniform religious belief; they didn't reject pluralism, but they believed the objective truths of the Bible were necessary to preserve the moral and religious foundation on which a thriving pluralism can exist.

• AND NOW—CONCERNING OBJECTIVE TRUTH:

America's Constitution was established to be the sole source of all government powers and to bar the concentration of powers and the enacting of arbitrary rules and processes. After the absolute power of kings was defeated in England and America, it revived in the Continent through Germany and Prussia. There, kingly prerogative power migrated to the bureaucratic administrative power of the states. This departure from the rule of law in favor of the prerogative power of government bureaucracies was admired and adopted by American academics and progressives who now see our Constitution as a barrier to enacting "Necessary" social justice.

Over the past 100 years, having rejected the objective truths of Natural Law, America has reestablished the very sort of prerogative bureaucratic power our Constitution strictly forbade. The long-standing justification, "it is necessary," for exerting prerogative power outside the law is recurring in modern American government.

In November 2014, President Obama officially announced he plans to issue Executive Orders that will act outside our laws and statutes governing immigration because Congress has failed to act. Ignoring the plain meaning of Article I, Section 1, of our Constitution ("All legislative Powers herein granted shall be vested in a Congress of the United

States"), he asserted that it is "Necessary" for him to exert his prerogative power that will be executed through bureaucratic agencies in the Executive Branch, rather than through lawful acts of Congress.

The Constitution ensures that government entities cannot be bureaucratized. The current American administrative state can only coexist with our Constitution if the rule of law is abandoned and objective truths are denied. Then Congress can surrender its lawmaking powers by delegating those powers to the bureaucracy, and still maintain its authority over the bureaucracy.

Congress has exchanged its lawmaking responsibilities to become an administrative oversight body, making Congress a major player in the politics of the administrative state. Most congressmen have come to prefer administration and regulation to the hard work of deliberation and legislation.

Jamie Whitten (Mississippi-D), was elected to the U.S. House of Representatives in 1941 and was re-elected for 25 more terms. He said, "The smartest thing we ever did was to throw the weight of the federal government behind local problems." That is, problems outside the Constitutional jurisdiction of government.

When the rule of law ceases to be the common standard of society, then their laws cease to be republican [based on the Constitution and objective truth] and become despotic [arbitrary laws, with no accountability to citizens or the Constitution]. Then freedom itself ceases to be an inalienable right and becomes a gift of government—or the fruit of effective lobbying of the privileged ruling class.

The problem is not the lobbyists or corporate contributors to political parties, it's the non-virtuous and self-privileged ruling class who, astonishingly, believe they are above the law. They are little kings who believe that kings are the law (the opposite of Rutherford's *Lex Rex—the Law is King*).

During a town hall meeting in August 2010, in Hayward, California, a constituent asked Congressman Pete Stark (D-CA) "If this [Obamacare] legislation is constitutional, what limitations are there on the federal government's ability to tell us how to run our private lives?" Congressman Stark's answer was disturbing but delivered unblinkingly: "I think there are very few constitutional limits that would prevent the federal government from rules that could affect your private life."

The questioner continued, "If [Congress] can do this, what can't they?" Stark's response reveals a fundamentally skewed view of government that is squarely opposed to the original intent of our Founders: "The federal government, uh, yes, can do most anything in this country."

Chapter Eleven—What shall we do?

Our future as a nation and culture hinges on objective truth:

There are three likely outcomes resulting from America's dangerous departure from objective truth, but only one possibility is rational:

1. The social/political pendulum will continue to swing in greater and greater extremes until chaos becomes normative in America.

2. Having no competent defenders, objective truth will be abandoned entirely. The Progressives win the ideological war: Tyranny is the inevitable result.

3. Objective truth is competently defended in the public arena of ideas. Objective truth re-engages in the Great American Social/ Political Debate. The security and happiness of citizens dramatically improve.

The Road to Chaos:

If objective truth is not engaged in the public debate, the status quo will result in increased tribalism in American culture—and in her streets. The absence of rational thinking rooted in objective truth will likely move the debate from a war of words to a war of weapons.

Dropping my car off to be serviced this morning, I saw a bumper sticker on an expensive car that advocated imprisoning all of our state and national Republican elected officials. No debate was wanted, just draconian force: imprison and silence the ideological opposition.

We must understand that silencing the opposition is the avowed tactic of American communist/socialists (refer back to Current Communist Goals, p14): "Infiltrate the press ... radio ... TV ... motion pictures;" "Discredit the Bible ... Founding Fathers ... the Constitution ... traditional American values."

We are currently experiencing the death of free speech in America. Conservatives risk being physically assaulted on college campuses. Just yesterday (October 8, 2018), the news reported two elderly men being accosted and abused by fascist ANTIFA members in Portland, Oregon because they were white men who tried to escape from the anarchists. The liberals who send death and rape threats to conservative women like Dana Loesch and Michelle Malkin have the same goal as ANTIFA. They want to use the threat of violence to convince them to quit speaking publicly and to intimidate other women who agree with them.

Internet giants are strategically censoring conservative media and promoting leftist media. Conservatives are being threatened and hindered from participating in public debates. Objective truth is unwanted and often prohibited in public debates. A great example of this is when James Damore at Google used an open forum to make scientifically supported arguments about women in STEM and then was fired for it. That's the perfect world for Progressives. They win by default without having to defend their arguments at all

As this decline unfolds, ordinary American's will conclude the protection of their lives, family members, their liberty, and property must become their personal responsibility and are forced to take the law into their own hands. The American tribes, the coalitions of victims, will be at war with each other. Like all tribes in history, they are united by their commonly held values and they will defend those values without regard for the society at large. The status quo in America is the Road to Chaos.

THE ROAD TO BUREAUCRATIC TYRANNY:

If objective truth is undefended and commonly rejected in American culture and governance, the Progressive definition of truth, that which works to accomplish the desired ends, will be the dominant ideology in social, economic, and political experimentations.

Students will continue to avoid books by dead white authors, men like Aristotle, Milton, Locke, Witherspoon, Hamilton, Washington, de Tocqueville, etc. A recent survey showed that less than 16% of current high school students have read one unassigned book in the last 12 months. The desire for selfish instant gratification is real: Scrolling Snapchat,

57

Googling, Netflix—how could difficult reading compete with these?

> "A new study has alarming findings but is probably not surprising to anyone who knows a teenager: High schoolers today are texting, scrolling and using social media instead of reading books and magazines. The reason for the concern is that the skill set and attention it takes to digest concepts in long-form writing are quite different from glancing at a text message or status update."

> "Reading long-form texts like books and magazine articles is really important for understanding complex ideas and for developing critical thinking skills." —by Hannah Natanson, *The Mercury News*, August 21, 2018.

We have raised multiple generations of students who are unable to reason, to think critically, and who have no basis in fact for their worldview and social-economic-political beliefs. The oft-criticized Millennials are not stupid, they're uneducated but thoroughly propagandized by progressive academic elites. When objective truth is denied then citizens are vulnerable to propaganda and sophistry; they will uncritically believe a lie.

Without the public defense of objective truth, the pathway is clear for increasing government control of every aspect of our lives. Welcome to George Orwell's "*1984*" dystopia.

Citizens apart from objective truth are incapable of self-government and self-determination. The bayonet will replace the Bible as the essential preventer of chaos. Our Constitution will be re-interpreted as the need requires. Unaccountable government bureaucracies will grow at the expense of the citizen's property and freedom.

But, who will oppose the unrestrained arrogance and expansion of power among the ruling elite? Truth is ignored and God's ancient warnings are no longer considered relevant:

> "We hope for light, but behold, darkness ... we grope along the wall like blind men ... we stumble at midday as in the twilight."

> "Denying the Lord ... and turning away from our God ... conceiving in and uttering from the heart lying words. Justice is turned back ... for truth has stumbled in the street and uprightness cannot enter. Yes, truth is lacking; and he who turns aside from evil makes himself a prey." —Isaiah 59:9-14.

America's future rests on whether we defend truth and oppose non-truth in the public arena of ideas. That defense must first be learned in our homes, then reinforced in our schools and churches. Without that preparation, the silent majority will remain silent. We, like drones, will plod down the Road to Bureaucratic Tyranny.

THE ROAD TO RECOVERY:

If we continue to battle with the symptoms and not the causes of America's cultural and political decline, we will simply become weary of our lack of progress and ultimately give up and adopt a protective citadel approach to our family life. Then the great American experiment will fail and it will be our fault.

It's important to understand that our's is primarily a battle of principles, not a political battle. It's doubtful there is any possible political solution to America's current decline. Where will we find the angels to be our government leaders? Without personal and public virtue, what politician will take the lead in restoring essential virtue in families and the citizenry and among our elected officials?

It's equally important to understand that the battle of principles must be fought in the arena of public ideas: In homes, neighborhoods, schools, in churches, in town-hall meetings, and the public media. The battle will require active and competent opposition to popular propaganda and academic sophistry. It is a battle that must be fought and either won or lost. Traditional American values and the objective truths of the Bible and Natural Law are worth fighting for. Our families depend on us to fight for their future.

CHAPTER TWELVE
WE NEED STRONG MEN:

Geoff Dench (1940-2018) was a British social scientist whose book, *Transforming Men*, challenged head-on the feminist model of gender relations and exposed its fatal flaws (give grace for the British spelling of some words):

"The feminisation of the state launches a new offensive in the gender war. It is now an orthodoxy that one of the primary duties of the state is to protect women's interests against men. Anna Coote and her colleagues (1990) write that fathers are no longer essential to the economic survival of family units. And Polly Toynbee (1989) can calmly incite women to forget about fatherhood and just look to the state for all the provisions needed to enable them to have careers and operate effectively without men. Quoting Toynbee: "What it (the state) can do is shape a society that makes a place for women and children as family units, self-sufficient and independent." —Geoff Dench, *Transforming Men*, 1996.

"It would not be overstating the case too much to suggest that it is the need of feminists for socialism which has kept the Left going for the last decade or longer. They are now surviving in the world ... by dint of political correctness, which treats attempts to unravel the social accounting of welfare as tantamount to the rape of defenceless women. But looking the other way will not prevent the current welfare state system from collapsing as a result of its own contradictions. Feminists have built their new palace on sand." — *ibid.*

In truth, what women and families need are wise, virtuous, and courageous men who will love them, protect them, and provide for their material, emotional and spiritual needs. Women and families need virtuous men, not female impersonators. And what children need most is mothering and fathering from good role models. Imagine the dire consequences if we fail to nurture boys into genuine manhood and girls into genuine womanhood. Look around you.

Males are designed to be the protectors and providers for their wives and children. Their broad shoulders, upper-body strength, and aggressive personalities, tempered by the tenderness of conscience taught by the principles of virtue, are the stuff noble warriors are made of. Men are meant to apply those natural attributes to specialized endeavors to provide for and protect their family, while women are meant to be generalists who apply their natural attributes to nurturing, training, and domesticating their family and community (including their husbands).

When the principles of virtue and Natural Law are abandoned, those male attributes become twisted from being the protector to being the predator of the weak. Undomesticated males are the most dangerous contributors to a chaotic society. God was right when He said, "It is not good for the man to be alone." — *The Bible*, Genesis 2:18.

In our traditional marriage vows, the man vows to assume all of the adult duties and responsibilities of a husband; the bride vows to assume all of the adult duties and responsibilities of a wife. Marital and parental roles and authorities are defined in the Bible's Natural Law. They are immutable principles that are necessary for a free and thriving society.

To reverse the slide of American families and culture into chaos, men must reclaim their roles in the family and society—they must aspire to become Noble Warriors. The Greek Noble Warrior was a mythical man who had all the virtues. What we mean by Noble Warrior is not a mythical man, but a real man who aspires to virtue and nobility of life. A man who aspires to be the kind of man his wife and children need; a man who is engaged in practically loving his wife and nurturing his children to maturity despite living in an environment hostile to virtue and faith. No corrupting strategy will be able to successfully resist his influences in the family and society. We and our families are desperate for such men.

CHAPTER THIRTEEN
WE NEED STRONG FAMILIES:

The biblical model for families is called the "nuclear family" because it forms the nucleus of every society—the fundamental building block of every civilization, out of which all other civil institutions arise. In its natural state, the family consists of a man and woman and their offspring children—the arrangement best suited to the nature of mankind and the nurturing of children. The nuclear family forms the healthiest and least costly environment in which to raise wholesome, well-adjusted children who have the best chance of becoming happy, productive citizens of the larger society. The biblical nuclear family is a proven superior model.

It's difficult to decide whether those who advocate and teach alternate forms for the family are incurably ignorant or just plain evil. Give a small place to ordinary common sense in debating family forms, and the God-designed traditional family wins hands down, every time. Nuclear families, as defined in Natural Law, have been around for quite a long time so examining a large sample to determine what works and what doesn't work is pretty straightforward. The statistics are in, and the Nuclear Family wins:

1. The father's direct involvement in his children's lives produces measurably positive outcomes. His absence, likewise, produces measurably negative outcomes for his family.

2. Children raised in two-parent homes (meaning a mother and father) are 82% less likely to live in poverty. The traditional family seems to be America's most powerful and least expensive weapon against poverty. Their children, typically, have a higher net worth, higher incomes, more household assets, and greater savings.

3. Children living with married parents are much less likely to become sexually active as teens or to give birth outside of marriage, regardless of race, ethnicity, or the parent's education.

4. Adolescents in intact families are considerably less likely to abuse alcohol or illicit drugs regardless of race, ethnicity, or family income. It seems the directive, "Just say no," works much better coming from parents than from billboards.

5. Adolescents living in intact families are much less likely to engage in the delinquent or anti-social behaviors that are plaguing American teens. Instances of male youth homicide are 95% more likely in communities with a high percentage of absent fathers. The main cause of inner-city crime is not poverty, it's broken families.

6. Children in intact families exhibit better emotional and psychological well-being. Children from broken families are more likely to engage in higher levels of anti-social behaviors, like running away from home,

school absence and suspensions, substance abuse, committing property crimes, violent behaviors, and being arrested, regardless of race, ethnicity, or parental education or income.

In the history of mankind, every nation that has distorted or abandoned the original design for the family has never prospered and most have self-destructed. The family in America is the target of flawed progressive ideologies that aim to replace the natural functions of families with government programs, administered by scientifically-trained experts. If the trend continues unopposed, our families, our culture, and our nation will be lost. Living in American will become a prison characterized by chaos, and there will be no escape.

Chapter Fourteen
We need strong churches:

A Great Debate, that is now largely decided wrongly in America, is whether religion is necessary for societal order.

This was not debated among the early Americans; it was a settled fact held in common by the culture. In the following quotations from some Founding Fathers, they were declaring the commonly-held beliefs of the citizens.

In their day, not one person would dare to dispute these assertions:

"And let us with caution indulge the supposition that morality can be maintained without religion. Whatever may be conceded to the influence of refined education on minds of peculiar structure, reason and experience both forbid us to expect that National morality can prevail in exclusion of religious principle." – George Washington, *Farewell Address*, 1796.

"Before any man can be considered as a member of Civil Society, he must be considered as a subject of the Governor of the Universe: And if a member of Civil Society, who enters into any subordinate Association, must always do it with a reservation of his duty to the general authority; much more must every man

67

who becomes a member of any particular Civil Society, do it with a saving of his allegiance to the Universal Sovereign."

— James Madison, *Memorial and Remonstrance Against Religious Assessments*, 1785.

"Once the government arrogates to itself the responsibility to nudge citizens into good behavior and foster good habits, it is acting less like a democratic government and more like a church—a church with armed police, tax collectors, and an army."

— Paul David Miller, *How Tocqueville Anticipated Our Culture Of Dependency*, February 21, 2014.

In our day, religion's role in societal order is hotly debated by Progressives, who see religion as a problem, not a solution:

"The Christian religion, as organized in its churches, has been and still is the principal enemy of moral progress in the world."

—Bertrand Russell, *Why I Am Not a Christian*, 1927.

"The state [not God] has the responsibility for creating institutions under which individuals can effectively realize the potentialities that are theirs." —John Dewey.

John Dewey expanded on the idea that, contrary to the Bible's teachings, human beings have no inherent nature or rights. According to Dewey, men are born as empty vessels, as nothing in themselves. As such, the individual becomes a product of his historical context. Dewey believed individuals are molded by the environment created by their government.

In 1840, de Tocqueville was astonished that uniquely in America "the spirit of religion and the spirit of freedom" were "intimately united and that they reigned in common over the same country."

He attributed religion's invaluable contribution to America's freedom to the common understanding of the separation of church and state as defined in Natural Law. In early America, family, religion, and government were functioning as co-equal and interdependent institutions—each with its own jurisdiction. He explained that, in America, religion was considered indispensable to self-governance and their republican form of government:

> "I do not know whether all Americans have a sincere faith in their religion – but I am certain that they hold it to be indispensable to the maintenance of republican institutions."

> "For the Americans the ideas of Christianity and liberty are so completely mingled that it is almost impossible to get them to conceive of the one without the other."
> —Alexis de Tocqueville, *Democracy in America*, 1840.

Those who would undermine a republic must first subvert their religion that teaches virtue and Natural Law, the foundations upon which their republic rests. That America's Founders, and the preponderance of its citizens, believed that religion was indispensable to the maintenance of freedom is indisputable.

The necessary and operating principles of freedom are found in the Bible's objective truth. In our day, that truth is being actively denied by those who would seek to enrich and empower themselves at the expense of the citizen's property and freedom.

De Tocqueville's conclusion in this matter of religion will serve to define for us America's political destiny:

> "Despotism may be able to do without faith, but freedom cannot."
> — Alexis de Tocqueville, *Democracy in America*, 1840.

This also, from Founding Father, John Jay, chosen the president of the Continental Congress in 1778, who was the first Supreme Court Justice, and who co-authored the Federalist Papers:

> "No human society has ever been able to maintain both order and freedom, both cohesiveness and liberty apart from the moral precepts of the Christian religion.... Should our Republic ever forget this fundamental precept of governance...this great experiment will then surely be doomed."

All of the disturbing pathologies of modern American culture find their root cause along one of two battle lines: Family and Religion. The members of intact traditional families and those with religious beliefs and practices tend to flourish; those who are outside of those historical norms tend to struggle and become dependent on government that is ill-suited to supply what should be provided by family and religion.

THE ROLE OF THE CHURCH:

In this fierce battle for the soul of American culture, the families cannot prevail on their own. The role and authority of the church must be allied with the family—both God-designed institutions must be properly functioning to check government usurpations and re-establish the principles of virtue and Natural Law as the basis for American society and government.

Most church members are feeding on spiritual Pablum when their teachers should be feeding them the Bible's rich objective Truth. The church's flocks are being carelessly shepherded, and thus, against God's warnings, are being blindly led and shaped by a corrupt culture (See Romans 12:1-2).

I can't remember the last time I heard a series of sermons on the biblical doctrine of Natural Law—and you probably can't either. Most church-goers today cannot even define Natural Law, nor could they point to the Bible's teachings of Natural Law. Yet these very teachings echoed from America's pulpits before and during the formative years of our nation, and those objective truths were commonly understood by American families.

Winston Churchill chose the hymn *Onward Christian Soldiers* for the church service when Churchill and President Franklin Roosevelt met in

1941 on the battleship HMS *Prince of Wales*. Afterward, he explained his choice in a radio broadcast: "We sang 'Onward, Christian Soldiers' indeed, and I felt that this was no vain presumption, but that we had the right to feel that we were serving a cause for the sake of which a trumpet has sounded from on high."

The "trumpet has sounded from on high" for the church to take up its God-assigned responsibilities for its members and families. There is a great need today for families to be taught, mentored, led by example, and joined in the battle for the soul of America by their local church leaders. Christians are not commanded to "take up the full armor of God ... having girded your loins with truth " to sit quietly in pews, listening to feel-good sermons while planning lunch (Ephesians 6:13-14).

If local churches continue to disregard their responsibility to "equip the saints for the work of the ministry" (Ephesians 4:12); if churches fail to equip men for virtuous leadership; if they fail to equip families to educate and model virtue and objective truth to their children; if they fail to model and teach virtue as a goal of life and God's objective truth as our final authority in faith and practice; if the local church continues to abandon their constituent families to being shaped by our dystopian culture, then don't expect the families to survive this onslaught of progressive non-truth to which they are subjected on every front every day.

If our families fail, and the church does nothing, we should lay the blame squarely on the church's doorstep. It is the church, not families, that God has commissioned to be "the pillar and ground of the truth" (1 Timothy 3:15). The church is the steward of objective truth. The church must teach and model objective truth. We need a renewed "Black Robed Regiment" to declare that old-time religion that stirred early Americans to cherish the Bible's objective truths. That is the real battleground for the soul of America.

www.ingramcontent.com/pod-product-compliance
Lightning Source LLC
Chambersburg PA
CBHW062103280526
45788CB00003B/1337